T0012305

UNUSUAL LiFe CYCLES OF

MAMMALS

by Jaclyn Jaycox

CAPSTONE PRESS
a capstone imprint

Capstone Captivate is published by Capstone Press, an imprint of Capstone.
1710 Roe Crest Drive
North Mankato, Minnesota 56003
www.capstonepub.com

Library of Congress Cataloging-in-Publication Data is available on the Library of Congress website.
ISBN: 978-1-4966-9560-4 (hardcover)
ISBN: 978-1-4966-9703-5 (paperback)
ISBN: 978-1-9771-5525-2 (eBook PDF)

Summary: Have you ever heard of a mammal that lays eggs? What about a mammal that can give birth to 50 babies at once? Young readers learn all about echidnas, Tasmanian devils, and other mammals with unusual life cycles.

Image Credits
Getty Images/Pool, 17; Minden Pictures/Suzi Eszterhas, 25; Newscom: Dave Watts/NHPA/Photoshot, 11, 27; Shutterstock: Eric Isselee, cover, Evelyn D. Harrison, 19, Hung Chung Chih, 29, Lua Carlos Martins, 15, Lukas_Vejrik, 9, Positive Snapshot, 23, SJ Watt, 13, teekayu, 21, Tiplyyashina Evgeniya, 5, udaix, 7
Design elements: Shutterstock: emEF, Max Krasnov

Editorial Credits
Editor: Gena Chester; Designer: Bobbie Nuytten; Media Researcher: Kelly Garvin; Production Specialist: Tori Abraham

Words in **bold** are in the glossary.

Printed and bound in China. PO4205

Table of Contents

CHAPTER 1

Mammal Life Cycle

What do dogs, bears, and humans have in common? They are all **mammals**! There are more than 5,000 kinds of mammals in the world. While many of these animals seem very different, they have a few things in common. Mammals have hair at some point in their lives. They are warm-blooded. This means that their bodies are able to maintain certain temperatures. Most give birth to live young. Most have the same life cycle. This is a series of changes that happen as animals grow.

Think of the life cycle of a dog. A dog gives birth to puppies. The puppies drink milk, or **nurse**, from their mother for the first few weeks of life. The mother takes care of them as they grow.

a Jack Russell terrier and her puppies

Dogs are in the puppy stage of life until they are around six to nine months old. Then they start the **adolescent** stage. It's like the teenage years for humans. They are no longer puppies, but not yet adults. They reach their adult stage at one year old.

Most mammals go through life cycles very similar to this. But there are a few with very different life cycles. Some lay eggs. Others have very short or very long **gestation** periods. And some have unique features that set them apart. Let's take a look at mammals with unusual life cycles.

A DOG'S LIFE CYCLE

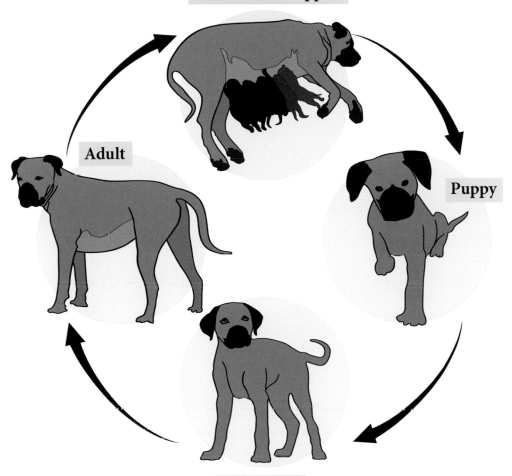

Mother and Puppies

Adult

Puppy

Adolescent

CHAPTER 2

Strange Births

Platypuses

A duck-billed platypus doesn't give birth to live young like other mammals. Instead, it lays eggs. A female digs a **burrow** and makes a nest in the ground. She usually lays two eggs. She keeps them warm and safe. After about 10 days, the eggs hatch.

Baby platypuses are very small. They drink milk from their mother. They stay in the burrow until they are about four months old. Then they leave the nest to go out and hunt on their own. They eat water animals like shrimp and crayfish. They eat insect larvae too. Once they're 12 to 18 months old, they are full-grown adults. They will begin to **mate** and lay eggs. Platypuses live for around 20 years.

Platypuses live only in Australia.

Echidnas

Echidnas, like platypuses, lay eggs. They have spiky fur on their backs and sides. Once a year, a female will lay one egg. She puts the egg in a pouch on her stomach. After about 10 days, the baby echidna hatches. It drinks milk from its mother. It stays warm and safe in her pouch for about two months. Then the baby starts growing its hair. It gets too spiky to stay in the pouch. The mother moves the baby to a burrow. She returns every few days to feed the young echidna. After about six months, the echidna is ready for life on its own. Echidnas can live more than 40 years in the wild.

LAYING EGGS

Echidnas and duck-billed platypuses are **monotremes**. They are the only mammals in the world that lay eggs. They may also be the world's oldest mammals.

a baby echidna in its burrow

Hippos

Hippos mate in the water. They are the only African land mammal to do this. They are also one of the only land mammals to give birth in the water. A hippo lives with other hippos in groups called **herds**. Female hippos carry their babies for about eight months before they give birth. They leave their herds just before giving birth. They usually have only one baby at a time.

The mother and baby hippo stay on their own for the first two weeks. After a few weeks, they both rejoin the herd. The herd protects the young hippo as it grows. Hippos are adults at about 8 years old. Then they leave their herds and mothers to find a mate. Hippos can live about 30 years in the wild.

Fact!

Baby hippos can nurse underwater. They close their nostrils and fold their ears shut.

a hippo and her young baby

CHAPTER 3

Unusual Pregnancies

Elephants

Elephants have the longest gestation periods of any mammal. Females carry their babies for almost two years! Mothers usually give birth to one baby. The baby is more than 200 pounds (100 kilograms) when it's born. It drinks milk from the mother for up to three years. When it has finished nursing, it becomes an adolescent.

Elephants live in herds. The herd helps protect young elephants. Other females in the herd help to raise them. Elephants become adults at around 12 years old. Males leave their mother to live alone or join another herd. Females stay with their mothers for life. Elephants can live about 60 years in the wild. Females usually have around four babies during their lifetime.

Elephants are the largest land mammals.

Rhinos

Rhinos are another mammal with long gestation periods. A female carries her calf for 16 months. The calf can walk and run about an hour after being born. It is born with hair. Rhinos live in Africa and Asia. These places can be hot during the day and cool at night. Rhino hair protects them from sunburn. It also keeps them warm at night.

A rhino calf starts eating plants at only a week old. But it will drink milk from its mother for at least a year. Males nurse longer as they will grow bigger as adults. Most adult rhinos live life alone, only coming together to mate. Females usually have calves every few years. Rhinos can live up to 50 years.

a rhino and her baby just after it's been born

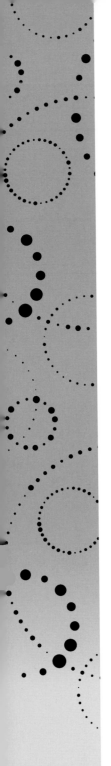

North American Opossums

North American opossums have the shortest gestation periods of any mammal in North America. They carry their young for 13 days! A female can birth up to 25 babies at a time. The babies are only as big as a bean. They must crawl up the mother's stomach and into her pouch. Usually less than half survive this journey.

Opossums nurse while in their mother's pouch. They grow quickly. They triple in size after just one week. When opossums are about two months old, they start to come out of the pouch. They stay with their mother, riding on her back for about three months. Then they are ready to go off on their own. Opossums can start mating at about six months old. They usually live up to two years.

Fact!

When opossums feel threatened, they lie on the ground, slow their breathing, and let their tongues hang out. **Predators** think the opossums are dead and walk away!

an opossum carrying her babies on her back

Chevrotains

Chevrotains are one of the smallest hoofed mammals. Females carry their young for six to nine months before giving birth. They have one baby at a time. The baby can stand on its own 30 minutes after being born. Mothers mate again quickly after this. Unlike other mammals after giving birth, they can get pregnant as little as 55 minutes later.

Female chevrotains don't stay with their young. But they visit them often for feedings. The young stay hidden on the forest floor. They stop drinking their mother's milk just before she gives birth again. Chevrotains are able to mate at about six months old. Females can spend almost their whole adult lives pregnant. Chevrotains can live about 12 years.

Fact!

Chevrotains have been around a long time. They are called "living fossils" because of how little they've changed in the last 30 million years.

Chevrotains are also called mouse deer.

CHAPTER 4

Different Bodies

Pangolins' bodies are covered in scales similar to reptiles. But don't let that fool you. These creatures are actually mammals! They are the only mammal in the world with scales. This tough skin helps to keep them safe. When they feel threatened, they curl up into a ball. Their scales act like spikes. It saves them from attacks from some of their biggest predators, including lions.

Pangolins also have unique tongues. Their tongues are not attached in their mouths like most other animals. Instead, it starts near the rib cage. When it's not in use, the tongue rolls up into its chest.

a pangolin protecting itself from attack

Pangolins usually live alone. They only come together to mate. Females make nests in burrows. Their gestation period lasts for three to five months. They usually give birth to one baby. Baby pangolins are called pangopups. Their scales are soft at first. But they start to harden by the second day.

Outside of the burrow, the baby rides on its mother's tail. The young pangolin starts eating insects. But it will drink milk from its mother for up to four months. Pangolins stay with their mothers for about two years. Then they are ready to have pangopups of their own.

ENDANGERED SPECIES

Pangolins are **endangered**. This means they are in danger of dying out. People hunt and capture them illegally. Their scales are used in medicines. Some people eat their meat. Over the last 10 years, it is estimated more than 1 million pangolins have been taken out of the wild. Some of those are in **captivity**. Others were killed by **poachers**.

Pangolins live in Africa, Asia, China, and India.

CHAPTER 5

High-Risk Babies

Tasmanian Devils

Tasmanian devils carry their young for about three weeks. Females can give birth to 20 or more babies. The babies are hairless and tiny. They race to the mother's pouch. Only the first four to make it there survive. The others don't have access to milk. This race for survival is unique to Tasmanian devils. The lucky four spend the next 100 days safely in the pouch. They eat and grow. Then the mother moves them to a den. She feeds them until they are about six months old. Young Tasmanian devils are fully grown and leave their mother after about nine months. They can live up to eight years.

a Tasmanian devil and her babies in their den

Giant Pandas

Giant pandas are anything but giant at birth. They weigh about 5 ounces (142 grams). Their eyes stay closed for about 50 days. They are hairless. They are the most helpless of all baby animals. Many do not survive.

Giant pandas have a very short breeding season. Females will mate only two or three days each spring. They give birth to one or two cubs. If two babies are born, only one will survive. The mother cares for the cub in a den. After about three months, the cub can crawl. At four months, it can run. It stays with its mother for about 18 months as it grows bigger and stronger. Then it leaves to eventually find a mate and repeat the life cycle.

a giant panda walking with her cub

Glossary

adolescent (ad-uh-LESS-uhnt)—a person in between childhood and adulthood

burrow (BUHR-oh)—a hole in the ground made or used by an animal; also, to dig

captivity (kap-TIV-ih-tee)—being kept or confined; animals are usually in captivity for their protection

endangered (in-DAYN-juhrd)—at risk of dying out

gestation (jus-TAY-shuhn)—the amount of time an unborn animal spends inside its mother

herd (HURD)—a large group of animals that lives or moves together

mammal (MAM-uhl)—a warm–blooded animal that breathes air; mammals have hair or fur; female mammals feed milk to their young

mate (MATE)—to join together to produce young; a mate is also the male or female partner of a pair of animals

monotreme (MAH-nuh-treem)—mammals that lay eggs; the platypus and echidna are the world's only monotremes

nurse (NURSS)—to drink mother's milk

poacher (POHCH-ur)—a person who hunts illegally

predator (PRED-uh-tur)—an animal that hunts other animals for food

Read More

Bozzo, Linda. *How Hippos Grow Up.* New York: Enslow Publishing, 2020.

Jacobson, Bray. *Mammal Life Cycles.* New York: Gareth Stevens Publishing, 2018.

Thomas, Isabel. *Elephant vs. Rhinoceros.* North Mankato, MN: Capstone Press, 2018.

Internet Sites

Ducksters: Mammals
www.ducksters.com/animals/mammals.php

Earth's Kids: Elephants
www.earthskids.com/ek-elephants.aspx

Kiddle: Life Cycle Facts for Kids
kids.kiddle.co/Life_cycle

Index

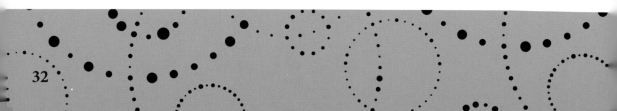